NEW BELIEVER'S SERIES

WATCHMAN NEE

THE DISCIPLINE OF THE HOLY SPIRIT

Living Stream Ministry
Anaheim, California

20

First Edition, November 1997.

ISBN 1-57593-976-2

Published by

Living Stream Ministry
2431 W. La Palma Ave., Anaheim, CA 92801 U.S.A.
P. O. Box 2121, Anaheim, CA 92814 U.S.A.

Printed in the United States of America

00 01 02 03 04 05 / 10 9 8 7 6 5 4 3 2

THE DISCIPLINE OF THE HOLY SPIRIT

Scripture Reading: Rom. 8:28; Matt. 10:29-31; Jer. 48:11; Gen. 47:7-10

We have believed in the Lord and have received a new life. But there are many habits which we acquired before we believed in the Lord. Many character traits and aspects of our disposition were part of us before we believed in the Lord. Those habits, character traits, and disposition have now become a frustration to the expression of the new life. This is the reason many people do not touch the new life or experience the Lord when they meet us. Often, others touch our old person. We may be very clever, but our cleverness is an unregenerated cleverness. We may be very warm, but that warmth is an unregenerated warmth. We may meet someone who is very gentle or very quick, but their gentleness and quickness are unregenerated gentleness and quickness. These old traits frustrate others from touching the Lord.

From the day we were saved, the Lord has been doing two things in us. On the one hand, He is tearing down our old habits, character, and disposition. This is the only way for Christ to express His life freely through us. If the Lord does not perform this work, His life will be frustrated by our natural life. On the other hand, the Holy Spirit is creating a new nature and a new character in us little by little, with its new living and new habits. The Lord is not only tearing down the old but also constituting us with the new. There is not only a negative tearing-down work, but also a positive constituting work in us. These are the two aspects of the Lord's work in us after our we are saved.

I. GOD BEING THE ONE WHO DOES THE WORK

After they are saved, many believers realize that their own person needs to be completely torn down. Yet they are too clever; they try to use artificial means to tear down their old nature, character, and habits. But the first thing God will tear down is our artificial means. Brothers and sisters, it is futile and even troublesome to use human energy to try to tear down the very nature, character, and habits which were built up by human energy in the past. We must realize from the very beginning that everything of the past must be torn down. But we cannot tear it down ourselves. Man's own effort to tear himself down will only result in outward adornment; it will only hinder the growth of the spiritual life. We do not need to tear ourselves down; God will do it for us.

We must be clear that it is God who wants to do this and God who does it. We do not have to come up with a way to deal with ourselves. God wants us to commit the entire work into His hands. We must be firmly impressed with this fundamental concept. God will work on us if He is merciful to us. God will order an environment that tears down our outward man. God knows how much there is that needs to be destroyed. He also knows our stubborn and strong spots. We may be too fast, too slow, too loose, or too legal in certain areas. Only God knows our need; no one else knows, not even ourselves. God is the only One who knows us thoroughly. We must allow Him to do the work.

In order to clarify the breaking and constituting work in us, we will use the phrase *the discipline of the Holy Spirit* for now. Although our whole environment is ordered by God, it is the Holy Spirit who applies this arrangement to us. God arranges the outward environment, but the Holy Spirit translates this arrangement into something inward and applies it to us. This conversion of outward events to inward experience is called the discipline of the Holy Spirit. Indeed, God orders the environment through the Holy Spirit; He does not order our lives directly but rather does so through the Holy Spirit. The dispensation between the Lord's ascension and His coming again is the dispensation of the Holy Spirit.

In this dispensation all of God's work is carried out through the Holy Spirit. The Holy Spirit arranges everything in the environment and provides inward guidance to God's children. There are a few passages in the book of Acts which say that the Holy Spirit prompted, stopped, and forbade. We call the environmental arrangements of the Holy Spirit and the inner prompting, stopping, and forbidding "the discipline of the Holy Spirit." This means that the Holy Spirit is disciplining us through all these experiences.

This discipline is not only for our guidance but also for our disposition. It involves not only our ways but also our character. We have a new life within us; the Spirit of God is dwelling in us. He knows what we need, and He knows the kind of experience that will bring us the most benefit. The discipline of the Holy Spirit is God's ordering of the proper environment through the Holy Spirit in order to meet our need and accomplish His work of breaking and constituting us. Thus, the discipline of the Holy Spirit destroys our natural disposition and habits and brings in the constitution of the Holy Spirit in maturity and in sweetness.

Our environment is altogether arranged by God. Even our hairs are numbered. If no sparrow falls on the ground without our Father's permission, how much more is our environment under His caring hand? A harsh word, an unkind gesture, a misfortune, an unfulfilled wish, a sudden loss of health, an abrupt departure of loved ones—all these are measured by the Father. Whether it be happiness, affliction, health, sickness, joy, or pain, everything that comes our way is approved by the Father. God arranges the environment for the purpose of destroying our old character and disposition and reconstituting us with a new character and disposition. God arranges the necessary environment for us, and unconsciously, we are broken and the Holy Spirit is constituted into us so that we acquire a character and disposition that resembles God. This God-like character and disposition will be expressed through us day by day.

As soon as we believe in the Lord, we should be clear about a few things: First, we need to be torn down, and then we need to be built up again. Second, we do not do the tearing-down and building-up work ourselves; God arranges the environment to tear us down and build us up.

II. HOW GOD ARRANGES EVERYTHING

How does God arrange everything for our good?

Everyone is different in nature, character, living, and habit. This is why we all need a different kind of breaking work. The kinds of discipline that God arranges are as varied as the number of people there are. Everyone is put into a different set of situations. A husband and a wife may be very close to each other, yet God will arrange a different environment for each of them. A father and a son, or a mother and a daughter, may likewise be very close to each other. Yet God arranges a different environment for each of them. In operating through our environment, God measures discipline to each one of us according to our individual needs.

Every arrangement of God is with the view of training us. Romans 8:28 says, "And we know that all things work together for good to those who love God, to those who are called according to His purpose." In Greek *all things* means "everything." *All* does not mean a hundred thousand things or even a million things. We cannot tell how big the number is. Everything, all things, are arranged by God for our good.

Therefore, nothing comes to us by accident. With us there is no coincidence. All things are arranged by God. From our point of view, our experience may seem confusing and puzzling; we may not see the intrinsic meaning behind everything, and we may not understand what it means. But God's Word says that all things work together for our good. We do not know what thing will bring us what kind of good. Neither do we know how many things are waiting for us and what good we will gain from them. But there is one thing we do know: Everything works together for our good. Nothing will happen to us that does not bring us good. We must see clearly that God's arrangement is to produce holiness in our character. We do not work out this holiness in ourselves; God is the One who creates this holy character in us through our environment.

One illustration will serve to explain how all things work together for our good. In Hangchow there are many silk weavers. Weaving involves many threads and colors. If one looks at the fabric from the back, everything seems to be a mess. An outsider will be puzzled; he will not know what pattern is on the other side of the fabric. But if he turns the fabric right side up, he will find beautiful figures, flowers, mountains, or rivers on it. Nothing is clear while the fabric is being woven; one sees only red and green threads moving back and forth. Likewise, our experience seemingly moves back and forth like a puzzle. We do not know what design God has in mind. But every "thread" which God uses, every discipline from His hand, has its function. Every color is there for a purpose, and the design is prearranged. God arranges our environment for the purpose of creating holiness in our character. Every encounter is meaningful. We may not be clear today, but one day we will be clear. Some of the things may not look that nice at the moment. But when we look back after some time, we will surely know why the Lord has done what He has done and what His purpose was for doing it.

III. OUR ATTITUDE

What should our attitude be when we face all these things?

Romans 8:28 says, "All things work together for good to *those who love God*." In other words, when God works, it is possible for us to receive the good, and it is also possible for us not to receive the good. This is quite related to our attitude. Our attitude even determines how soon we will receive the good. If our attitude is right, we will receive the good immediately. If we love God, everything that is of God will work for our good. If a man claims that he has no choice of his own, that he asks nothing for himself, and that he only wants everything that God gives to him, he should have only one desire in his heart—to love God. If he loves the Lord in his heart, all of the things around him will work together in love and for his good, no matter how confusing they may seem.

When something happens to us and we do not have the love of God within us, when we crave and seek things for ourselves, or when we pursue private interests apart from God, the good that God has reserved for us will not come. We are very good at complaining, struggling, murmuring, and groaning about many things. Brothers and sisters, please bear in mind that although all things do work together for good, we will not receive the good immediately if our hearts do not love God. Many of God's children have indeed encountered many problems, but they have not received any good. They experience much discipline, and God has arranged many things around them, but these things do not result in any riches on their part. The only reason for this poverty is that they have other goals besides God. Their hearts are not pliable towards God. They do not feel God's love; neither do they love God. They have a wrong attitude. As a result, they may have received many dealings, yet nothing remains in their spirit.

May God be merciful to us that we learn to love Him from our hearts as soon as we become Christians. Being short in knowledge does not mean much, because the way to know God lies in love, not in knowledge. If a man loves God, he will know God even though he may lack knowledge. However, if he knows much but does not love God in his heart, all of his knowledge will not help him to know God. There is a good line in one hymn: "To bring thee to thy God, / Love takes the shortest route" (*Hymns,* #477). If a man loves God, whatever he encounters will turn out to his good.

Our heart must love God, and we must learn to know His hand and humble ourselves under it. If we do not see His hand, our eyes will be distracted by men. We will feel that others are wrong or have betrayed us. We will feel that our brothers, sisters, siblings, parents, and friends are all wrong. As we condemn everyone, we fall into disappointment and disillusion ourselves, and nothing works to our good. When we say that the brothers and sisters in the church are all wrong and that nothing is right and everything is wrong, we are gaining nothing for ourselves except anger and criticism. If we remember the Lord Jesus' word, that "not one of them will fall to the earth apart from your Father" (Matt. 10:29), and if we realize that everything is of God, we will humble ourselves under His hand and receive the good.

Psalm 39:9 says, "I was dumb; I did not open my mouth; / For You have done this." This is the attitude of one who obeys God. Because God has done it and because God has allowed it to come upon us for our good, we humble ourselves and say nothing. We will not say, "Why did that happen to others, and why is this happening to me?" When we love God and know His hand, we will not open our mouth. In this way we will witness God's breaking and constituting work in us.

Some may ask, "Should we accept everything from Satan's hand too?" The basic principle is that we will take whatever God allows to come upon us. As for attacks from Satan, we have to resist.

IV. BREAKING AND CONSTITUTING

The Lord causes many things to come our way, few of which are according to our preference. This is why the Bible charges, "Rejoice in the Lord always" (Phil. 4:4). We should rejoice in the Lord. This is the only way we can rejoice always. Besides the Lord, what can make us rejoice always? Why does God allow all the bad things to come upon us? What is His purpose for doing these things? His goal is to break down our natural life. If we read Jeremiah 48:11, we will be clear.

Jeremiah 48:11 says, "Moab has been at ease from his youth; / And he is settled on his lees / And has not been emptied from vessel to vessel; / Nor has he gone into exile. / Therefore his taste remains in him, / And his scent is not changed." The Moabites were the descendants of Lot (Gen. 19:36-37). They were related to Abraham but were of the flesh. Moab was at ease from his youth and never experienced any tribulation, trial, blow, suffering, or pain. Nothing happened to him that would cause him to shed tears; nothing ever rent his heart or frustrated his way. In man's eyes this is such a blessing. But what did God say about the Moabites? He said, "He is settled on his lees / And has not been emptied from vessel to vessel." For wine to settle on its lees means that the liquid is a mixture. When wine ferments, the top part becomes clear liquid, while the lees sink to the bottom. As soon as the vessel is shaken, the lees and the liquid mix together again. In order to have a clear liquid, one has to pour the wine from one vessel to another. In the old days there was no filter, and the only way to remove the lees was to pour the liquid from one vessel to another. The liquid and the lees were originally mixed together. By pouring the liquid from one vessel to another, the lees were left behind. Sometimes some lees would escape with the liquid to the other vessel, and there would be the need to pour the liquid to yet another vessel. This would go on and on until all the lees were gone. Moab was never emptied from one vessel to another. He was like wine settled on its lees. His "lees" were not yet removed. This is why it says that "his taste remains in him, / And his scent is not changed." Moab always tasted like Moab. His scent remained the scent of Moab. His condition had not changed since the first day. But God is not after the old scent. He wants to change the scent.

Some have been believers for ten years, yet their taste remains the same as it was ten years ago. They are like Moab, whose taste remained and whose scent was not changed. Some people were sloppy when they first believed in the Lord. After twenty years they are still sloppy. They lived in ignorance and foolishness the first day, and they still live in ignorance and foolishness today. Their taste remains the same, and their scent is not changed. God does not want this. God wants to remove our old habit, nature, and character; He wants to remove every undesirable element in us. He wants to empty us from this vessel to that vessel and from that vessel to another vessel. After being emptied a few times, our "lees" will be left behind, and the original taste will be gone.

Moab had an easy life, but as a result, "his taste remains in him, / And his scent is not changed." Perhaps our life is not as easy as Moab's. Perhaps we have not been "at ease from ... youth." Perhaps we have had to go through "many tribulations" like Paul (Acts 14:22). If so, we should realize that the Lord is removing our lees and our original taste. The Lord wants to take away our own taste and natural scent. The old things must be torn down. The Lord has to uproot them all. He is pouring us from one vessel to another and then to a third. He allows this to happen to us today and that to happen to us tomorrow. The Lord turns us from one environment to another, from one experience to another. Each time He arranges an environment around us and breaks us, we will shed some of our old taste and scent. Time after time we will be purified of our old taste. Every day we will be a little different than the day before, and the next day we will be different still further. This is the way the Lord works in us; He tears down a little today and a little tomorrow, until all our lees are gone, our taste is lost, and our scent is changed.

God is not only breaking us on the negative side but also constituting us on the positive side. From the life of Jacob in Genesis, we can see the meaning of constitution.

Jacob's life began from a low point. He struggled with his older brother in his mother's womb and strove to be the first-born by holding on to his brother's heel. He was crafty and greedy, always deceitful and taking advantage of others. He deceived his own father, brother, and uncle. But in the end he was deceived by his uncle and his sons. He tried his best to prosper, but in the end he found himself in a famine. We can say that Jacob's way was fraught with suffering. Some people spend their lives in ease and comfort, but Jacob's life was full of affliction.

While he was going through his sufferings, God was breaking him down again and again. He suffered one thing after another. Every experience he went through was a suffering to him. But thank God, after going through so much suffering in His hand, he finally acquired a touch of God's holiness. We see this when he was in Egypt. There we see a gentle, humble, bright, and dignified man. He was so meek and humble that he could ask for grace and mercy from his son. Yet he was so crystal clear that he could utter prophecies which Abraham could not utter. He could give blessings which Isaac could not give. He was so dignified that even Pharaoh bowed his head to receive his blessing. This shows us that through God's breaking work, the lowly Jacob had become someone God could use. Jacob had become a man of God!

After years of breaking, God constituted Jacob with Himself. This is why we can see such a beautiful picture at Jacob's deathbed when he leaned on the top of his rod and worshipped God. Though he was sick in bed, he could still lean on the top of his staff and worship God. This proves that he still remembered his pilgrim life and had not given up his pilgrim characteristic. At first he struggled to sit up, put his feet down by the bed, and prophesied. After prophesying, he gathered up his feet, gave up his breath, and died. The way he died was beautiful! This is indeed a beautiful picture.

We can muse carefully upon the whole life of Jacob. At the time he was born, I am afraid no one had a worse "taste" than he had. But when he left the world, his old taste was gone altogether. What we see is a man fully constituted by God.

We must realize that everything that comes upon us is for our edification one way or another. God tears us down through all kinds of sufferings. The tearing down can be quite painful. But after we pass through these trials, something will be constituted into us. In other words, when trials arise, it may appear that we are failing, but His grace will always carry us through. In the process of overcoming our trials, something is wrought into us. As we overcome our trials again and again, the constitution within us grows day by day. On the one hand, God puts us through difficult circumstances and tears us down through our trials. On the other hand, something is added into us as we rise from our trials.

Thank God that we have the discipline of the Holy Spirit. May God have mercy on us. May He break us and constitute us through the discipline of the Holy Spirit so that we may reach maturity.